A Portrait of Dean

This portfolio of personal photographs, sometimes stylised and idiosyncratic, reflects many of the diverse features that make the Forest special. Having already published a book featuring the old iron and coal industries, I wanted to paint a broader picture here; but no portrait of Dean can ignore the area's rich industrial past and mining is again featured in these pages.

Some of these images have already appeared in the *Forest Frontiers* exhibition at Dean Heritage Centre, and some in *Landscape & Legacy* at the Forester Gallery (both in 2002); many have been taken since. My previously stated view that a photograph needs only enough information to tell its story is often supported here by impressionistic renditions.

My Forest boundaries are the two big rivers, the Severn and the Wye, and the Gloucester–Ross section of Telford's Milford Haven road, the modern A40; only a couple of locations fall outside this definition of Dean. The book is divided into three 'chapters': 'On the Edge', 'Under the Canopy' and 'Continuum'

– but these are loose headings, and many images could fit comfortably in more than one category.

'On the Edge' follows the perimeter of the Forest, though not in a strict geographical order; 'Under the Canopy' gets into the heart of the woods and 'Continuum' speaks for itself, underlining the fruits of human endeavour and often featuring fathers and sons. Some pages follow a thematic sequence, but the pairs of photographs are linked visually as much as by subject.

I would like to thank those who agreed to be photographed, and all who assisted me with this book, including Forest Enterprise, and especially Paul Manning for helping me to select and lay out the photographs and Edna Healey, herself a 'daughter of Dean', for generously contributing the foreword.

Chris Morris
Autumn 2003

High Woolaston: sheep fair at Tidenham Chase *(see also back cover)*

A PORTRAIT OF DEAN

Photos from the Forest

Chris Morris

with a foreword by

Edna Healey

TANNER'S YARD PRESS

To Malcolm, Mike and Tony, who taught me photography

First published 2003 by Tanners Yard Press
Church Road, Longhope, Gloucestershire GL17 0LA

Introduction © Edna Healey 2003
© 2003 Chris Morris

Designed by Paul Manning
Printed and bound in Great Britain by The Charlesworth Group,
Huddersfield, West Yorkshire

British Library Cataloguing in Publication Data
A catalogue record for this book is available from the British Library

ISBN 0-9542096-2-1

Published with the support of the Forest of Dean
Integrated Rural Development Programme

The
Countryside
Agency

Foreword

This book of photographs by Chris Morris has given me the deepest pleasure.

It was sent to me at a particularly appropriate time when I was struggling to catch in words the unique magic of the Forest of Dean for the first chapter of my autobiography. I was myself born in the Forest, in Coleford, of at least three generations of Foresters, so the subjects of these photographs have a special resonance for me.

I remember with delight the first wild snowdrops in the woods, the trees frosted in winter. I too have been pulled across the lucid waters of the Wye in a shallow boat by the overhead chain. I have biked and hiked my way through the Forest green rides. Like Chris, I have often seen the clump of trees sunlit on a distant hill, the single wild plum tree in the wooded glade, and the sea of blue under the spring trees. For me there have never been bluebells like those in the Forest.

All this beauty Chris has caught with great sensitivity. But his great talent is in the art of contrast: he brings together the ugly and the beautiful to make a surprisingly powerful impact, as, for example, a sheet of corrugated iron lying at an angle before a church steeple. For these are no conventional chocolate-box country landscapes: here there are coal tips, old iron workings and tin-roofed huts, half hidden by the brambles and tall green bracken. I find his iridescent foxglove, erect before the overgrown old tram road, profoundly moving.

Chris catches with skill and understanding the character in the faces of his free miners in front of their mine, their strength and humour, and the simple directness of the little congregation outside their tin chapel.

I am not competent to judge his photographic technique, but I particularly like the distant views seen through shifting mist, as they so often are in the Forest. My husband, Denis Healey, himself an excellent photographer, found these photographs 'very good indeed', and said 'Chris Morris is no ordinary photographer'. And I wholeheartedly agree.

Edna Healey

ON THE EDGE

*'On down the row, the woods getting close
and the secret shade'*
William Faulkner

Above May Hill: Christmas, view to the Severn

Over: the Severn in flood at Telford's bridge

Right Bullo Pill on the Severn: harbour steps

Facing page Awre: a rank of disused salmon 'putchers' *(see page 93)*

Right Minsterworth: the Severn Bore

Facing page Purton: abandoned barges

The Wye at Chepstow

Below A remnant of Brunel's railway bridge

Right A woodworker's ripsaw by Rennie's road bridge

Facing page The river below the castle

Above Bigsweir bridge: detail

Right Tintern Abbey

Facing page Bigsweir bridge:
Offa's Dyke path by the Wye

Facing page Symonds Yat hand ferry

Above Lea: plough and pasture

Facing page Weston: mist on
Penyard Hill

Left Longhope: the view to May Hill

Facing page May Hill, the summit grove: Scots pines planted for Victoria's Golden Jubilee in 1887

Facing page May Hill: after a visit to the cider house

Right Churcham: the view to May Hill

UNDER THE CANOPY

'Even Gods have lived in the woods like me'
Virgil

Above Beechenhurst, the Forest Sculpture Trail:
'Searcher' by Sophy Ryder

Above Snowdrops at Coleman's Wood

Right Longhope: composite featuring aspects of village history

Right Cannop pond: dew on trees

Facing page Nottwood Hill: plum blossom

Right Sallowvallets: frost on saplings

Facing page Cannop pond

Right Coleman's Wood: catkins

Facing page Mallards Pike Lake

Right Cannop Valley: a lone plum tree on the site of the Speculation Colliery reminds us that here were miners' cottages and gardens

Facing page Brinchcombe: a view from Staple Edge

Above Brockhollands

Facing page The Severn at
Newnham: view from Blaize Bailey

Left New Fancy

Facing page Soudley

Right Mirystock: winding chain on
Waterloo middle tip

Facing page Steam Mills: Haywood
Level

Right Longhope: willow tunnel

Facing page Mirystock bridge and tunnel: on the route of the Lydbrook branch of the Severn & Wye Railway

Left Moseley Green

Facing page Devil's Chapel: scowles, ancient iron workings, with orienteering marker

CONTINUUM

'Keep on keeping on'
Bob Dylan

Above Cannop: Mark and Mervyn Bradley, still producing coal at Monument
Mine, assisted by Richard Jennings, Reg Preece and Jake the dog

Right Sallowvallets: Forest closure during the Foot and Mouth epidemic

Facing page Nailbridge: Remembrance Day at Holy Trinity, Drybrook (the Forest Church)

Left Hopes Hill

Facing page Littledean: checking for contamination after sheep disposal during Foot and Mouth

Right Sallowvallets: sheep and 'badger', back in the woods after Foot and Mouth

Facing page Sallowvallets: ramblers

Cannop: view from Sallowvallets. The Cannop Colliery waste tips rearing up through the trees serve as a monument to the sweat and endeavour that produced them.

Right Parkend: stone gateposts

Facing page Cannop: workers in the stone factory

Left The Kymin, high above the Wye at Monmouth, was originally built as a gentlemen's dining club. When Nelson visited in 1802 he was mixing pleasure with business. His travelling companions were Lord and Lady Hamilton; his business was selecting Forest oaks for the navy.

Facing page Plump Hill: winter oak

Right Speech House: leaning oak

Facing page Moseley Green: modern forestry equipment strips, grabs, fells and slices in one operation.

In autumn 2001 Forest Enterprise, in partnership with the Countryside Agency, set up an experimental scheme to supply local woodworkers with oak produced from Forest thinnings, that would otherwise have been pulped. Shown here are three of the thirty-five participants in the 'Forest Oak Project'.

Right Staunton: Gilbert Crawford and Mervyn Bic of Belbic Design

Facing page Yorkley: Ross Brimson

Left Longhope: Peter Walwyn

Right Blakeney: Glynn Bullock, community officer for Forest Enterprise, at number 14 Forest marker stone

Facing page Mirystock: Waterloo western tip

Left Collafield: lime kilns, restored by Forest Enterprise

Facing page Bream: Princess Royal Colliery tips

Right Bream: Princess Royal Bath House was due for demolition, despite arguments for its social and architectural importance. This image was originally made as a requiem, but two weeks before the February 2003 deadline the building was granted a reprieve.

Facing page Bream: reunion of ex-Princess Royal miners in front of the derelict colliery offices. Chatting over old times, old comrades, dusty lungs and compensation claims, they voice unanimous approval for the restoration of the Bath House.
From left: Denis Hoare, Don Johnson (chairman of the Freeminers Association), Horace Jones and Ryan Saunders.

Right Soudley: Zion Baptist Chapel, as square and solid as an engine house, is now in the care of Dean Heritage Museum Trust.

Facing page Plump Hill: Fairplay Shaft engine house (due to be restored by Forest Enterprise)

Right Whitecliff: eighteenth-century iron furnace, of national importance, owned by Dean Heritage Museum Trust

Facing page St Briavels Castle, now a youth hostel

74

Right Mitcheldean: view from Plump Hill

Facing page Edge End: Methodist Chapel, congregation after Sunday service

Right Abenhall: view to May Hill

Facing page Edge End: New Found Out mine

Left Cannop: many former rail routes are now cycle tracks

Facing page Norchard: headquarters of Dean Forest Railway

Right Soudley: cider mill at Dean Heritage Centre

Facing page Lea: apple orchard

Right Clearwell: Ray and Jonathan Wright mine and sell ochre. The ancient iron ore caverns are open to the public.

Facing page Blaize Bailey: Ray and Andy Tosh, cider-makers

Above Clearwell: iron headframe over iron mine shaft

Facing page Beechenhurst: 'Cathedral' by Kevin Atherton on the Forest Sculpture Trail

Left and right Longhope

Facing page Lydbrook: the Wye in flood

Left Blakeney: bringing in orienteering markers after a race

Facing page Moseley Green: Cinderford Band, playing at the Rising Sun

Right Birdwood: Diana Smart,
prize-winning cheese-maker

Facing page Awre: Chris and Chris
Cadogan, salmon fishermen

Left Coleford: Karaoke at the
King's Head

Facing page Cinderford:
Dave Bradley, rugby coach,
with the Under-14s at Dockham
Road

Longhope: Tanners Yard

Other books by Chris Morris published by Tanners Yard Press

Work in the Woods
Dean's Industrial Heritage

Under Blorenge Mountain
Blaenavon Industrial Landscape